Medusa

Medusa

From the Amazon's Bestselling Author
Nandini Sahu

BLACK EAGLE BOOKS
Dublin, USA | Bhubaneswar, India

Black Eagle Books
USA address:
7464 Wisdom Lane
Dublin, OH 43016

India address:
E/312, Trident Galaxy, Kalinga Nagar,
Bhubaneswar-751003, Odisha, India

E-mail: info@blackeaglebooks.org
Website: www.blackeaglebooks.org

First International Edition Published by
Black Eagle Books, 2025

Medusa (Poems)
by **Nandini Sahu**

Copyright © Nandini Sahu

All rights reserved. No part of this publication may be reproduced, stored in a retrieval system, or transmitted, in any form or by any means, electronic, mechanical, photocopying, recording or otherwise without the prior permission of the publisher.

Cover Art: **Parthasarathi Sahu**
Interior Design: Ezy's Publication

ISBN- 978-1-64560-693-2 (Paperback)
Library of Congress Control Number: 2025938134

Printed in the United States of America

Dedicated
to
'You'.

You traced the shadows in her scales,
a tale entwined in cursed veils.
Through frozen whispers, lost in time,
you heard the ache beneath the chime.
You stirred the breezes within her chest,
unshackled myths the world suppressed.
Her voice, once silenced, learned to rise
like a raging tide in a flaming sky.
Firm you stand, a sculpted vow
stirring the big wind
of the 'écriture féminine'.
A beacon then, unyielding now,
her muse, her myth, her whispered plea,
bound beyond infinity,
'You'.

Preface

My tenth poetry collection, *Medusa*, problematizes the Quixotic idea of the dichotomy between the perfect women as put on a pedestal by the society and the real women of flesh and blood with all her insecurities and follies. Majority of the poems are about the inlet of accepting the construct of the perfect Muse and the unending search for it.

Medusa represents philosophy, beauty and art. Likewise, *Medusa*, this poetry collection, is about an individual's life philosophy, artistic desires, his/her contentment and hurts. Through these poems, like Hemingway, I want to "Write hard and clear about what hurts.", thus, I write poetry of humankind, for "the atom belonging to me as good belongs to you"(Whitman). Like Rumi, the poems whisper at you, "The breeze at dawn has secrets to tell you. Don't go back to sleep." Reiterating Gibran's powerful words, the poems claim, "A truth can walk naked. But a lie needs to be dressed." Yet, with Sartre, I realize, "Every word has consequences, every silence too"; thus, I take the responsibility, accountability of every word that I write in this poetry book.

The radical title *Medusa* poses an elemental question, why *Medusa*? What is the Indian context of the title? To answer that question, let me attempt to define the personae and the personification of *Medusa* first, then go to the Indian context or otherwise.

The Myth of *Medusa*, one of the most iconic tales in Greek mythology, weaves a tale of beauty, betrayal and transformation. *Medusa* was once a mortal woman of extraordinary beauty. Among her most captivating features was her golden hair, which seemed to shimmer like sunlight. She served as a priestess in Athena's temple, a sacred position that demanded purity and devotion. Her beauty, however, drew the attention of gods and mortals alike, and her beauty became her curse. This may remind the Indian reader of Indra Dev who was enamoured by the bathing beauty, Ahalya, the wife of Rishi Goutam, and came to her in disguise and violated her body. The sea god Poseidon, overwhelmed by his desire for *Medusa*, pursued her relentlessly. One day, in Athena's temple, Poseidon violated *Medusa*. This desecration of her sacred space infuriated Athena. Yet, instead of punishing Poseidon, Athena turned her wrath upon *Medusa*. In her divine anger, Athena transformed *Medusa* into a creature feared by all---her once-lustrous hair became writhing snakes, her eyes gleamed with a curse so powerful that whoever met her gaze turned instantly to stone. Banished and reviled, *Medusa* fled to the desolate island of Sarpedon and she lived in isolation. *Medusa* was not alone in her monstrous form. She became one of the three Gorgons, though unlike her immortal sisters, Stheno and Euryale, *Medusa* remained mortal. Her vulnerability, paired with her deadly gaze, made her both pitied and feared. Folktales write, she is under a curse which causes everything she looks at to turn to stone. And some other popular lore credits *Medusa* to be a symbol of protection. *Medusa* is a part of the huge intertwining, intertextual, polyphonic stories of ancient Greek mythology. Because *Medusa*'s head was placed on Athena's shield and her blood was revealed to hold the power of both life and death, her head became a symbol of protection. *Medusa* was one of the three Gorgons, daughters of Phorcys and Ceto, sisters of the Graeae, and Ladon--all dreadful and formidable beings. A beautiful mortal, she was the exclusion in the family, until she incurred the wrath of Athena, due to her ill-fated rendezvous with destiny.

Medusa's story intersects with that of Perseus, the son of Zeus and Danaë. Tasked by King Polydectes with bringing back the head of *Medusa*—a feat envisioned to be impossible---Perseus embarked on his perilous quest. Aided by Athena and Hermes, Perseus received gifts to aid him: a mirrored shield, winged sandals, a harped sword, and Hades' helm of invisibility.

Perseus found *Medusa* asleep in her lair, surrounded by the petrified remains of those who had come before him. Using the mirrored shield to avoid her deadly gaze, he approached carefully and severed her head with the Harpe sword. From her blood sprang the winged horse Pegasus and the golden giant Chrysaor, her children by Poseidon, born from her severed neck.

Even in death, *Medusa*'s power, her legacy, endured. Perseus used her head as a weapon to defeat enemies, including the sea monster Cetus, to rescue Andromeda. Eventually, he presented the head to Athena, who placed it on her aegis, a shield that symbolized divine protection and terror. *Medusa*'s tragic story is presented as a tale of gender bias in this poetry collection; but also, in some poems, *Medusa* metaphor stands for gender harmony, women empowerment and feminine-unabashed-uninhibited-desires. Once a mortal of great beauty and innocence, *Medusa* was punished not for her sins but for her victimhood. Her transformation into a monster reflects themes of divine caprice, mortal suffering and the consequences of unchecked power. In death, *Medusa* became a paradox; a symbol of fear and power, of vengeance and victimhood, her story enduring as a poignant reminder of the complexities in Greek mythology.

The flag and emblem of Sicily features *Medusa*'s head. Two species of snakes contain her name, the venomous pit viper Bothriopsis-medusa and the nonvenomous snake called Atractus-medusa. In Greek folktales, *Medusa* is also called as Gorgo, was one of the three monstrous Gorgons, generally described as a winged human woman with living venomous snakes in place of her hair.

According to The Met Museum, *Medusa* is portrayed in most Greek art as an "apotropaic symbol used to protect and ward off the negative," representing a "dangerous threat meant to deter other dangerous threats, an image of evil to repel evil." In modern tales of Gorgon, she is a symbol of female rage. *Medusa* prayed to Athena for guidance and forgiveness for the sins that she never committed, like Ahalya remained a cursed stone for ages for the sins that she never committed. Athena cursed *Medusa* for betraying her. *Medusa* was sent to a faraway island and was cursed so that no man would want her, thus, she was a victim who was blamed. But in the contemporary cultural imagination, *Medusa* is perceived as a powerful symbol of feminine power, beauty, intelligence and wisdom, associated with the goddess Metis, who was the wife of Zeus. The snake-like head is a symbol of her astuteness, a distortion of the matrifocal ancient goddess who the Greeks must destroy. *Medusa*'s divine powers are called 'Trichokinesis'. *Medusa* possesses prehensile, gasping hair, and she can not just control the growth and movement of it, but can maneuver each strand exclusively. Unrestrained, her tougher-than-steel hair is elementally more than six feet long. She maintains this control even when the hair has been cut from her head.

A lot of magical realism here, isn't it?

In any case, *Medusa* has a larger than life image in world literature. *Medusa* is benevolent, yet astute, kind, compassionate, yet forbidding. She is the regular, here-and-now, normal woman with all the strengths and weaknesses in her multi-layered, multifaceted character, like us modern, post-modern and post-post-modern women, hence this title of my book!

If the readers find a facet of femininity in most of these poems, it is of course quite natural. After all, providentially, I am a woman! Regarding the artistic merits of the poems in this collection, I think gender does play a role, but that is not the only theme. In fact, to even voice such a submission is unscrupulous. It is natural that as a woman, because of my physical, emotional and spiritual inclinations, I might have given certain issues greater consideration through these poems, issues that men may not usually address. Yet, like Rumi, I believe, "The flute is totally empty. It is he breath that flows through, sings and dances. To be empty is not emptiness." Thus, some poems in this collection speak quietly, but they give the message loud and clear.

I believe that if those who choose creative writing, especially poetry, to express their inner selves, feel they have to do so with their gender in their cognizance, they would never evolve in their creativity -- and that is not a welcome situation. Thus, when I write, if I keep discerning, oh I am a woman and I have to address feminine issues rather than anthropoid issues, then that is a kind of bringing myself to a standstill and self-destruction. Because what substances, is to nurture and nourish one's own constructive geographies until one reaches a level worthy of being human and humane. Ultimately, what is important is the work produced by a human being and not one labelled as a man or a woman or queer, for that matter. When a poem reaches a certain level of maturation, it separates itself from its creator and connects to a larger world where it is valid based on its own merits. What matters is not the artist marked as man or woman, but the work itself--a creation that transcends labels and stands as a testament to the human spirit. When a poem reaches its zenith, its highest artistic merit, it unbinds itself from its maker, rising to a realm where it is judged not by the hands that birthed it, but by the truth it carries, the beauty it breathes, and the world it unveils.

Well, after I had written all the poems, when I gave a cursory look at the poems, one by one, poem after poem, I realized, "Everything that irritates us about others can lead us to an understanding of ourselves." (Carl Jung) With these poems, I move one step forward to self-realization. I understand my weaknesses, feebleness, my follies, Yet, the next moment, I count my blessings. Then, I love being a woman, a passionate, fervent woman, I understand the layers of my character, thus, human character. I value the green culture, ocean humanities, sound culture, Anthropocene and the culture of compassion, I write about those pertinent issues in these poems.

With immense happiness, I offer *Medusa* to my readers and wait for their reaction to the poems.

Nandini Sahu
Kolkata, Spring 2025

Acknowledgements

A book is a voyage; and the journey is fascinatingly electrifying if it's a poetry collection like *Medusa*, with many poems close to the poet's heart. The journey of *Medusa,*, most poems being close to my heart, has been shaped by the echoes of my past, the undertones of the present and the revelations of the future.

I would like to express my gratitude to many people as I designate *Medusa* to take a tangible birth and I send her to the world of the black and white.

To my readers--you give life to these pages; you are the seekers who make my poetry a shared voyage. Your engagement, reflection and curiosity are the true rewards of *Medusa*.

To my publisher from BEB, Shri Satya Pattanaik, your faith has turned my thought into text, my poetic vision into reality. And to Mr.Ashok Parida, for taking care of the finesse of the printing and publishing.

To my students and researchers, particularly Sagar, Bhaskar and Devendar, for reading some of the *Medusa* poems with keen interest much before they are published.

To my family, and to my mentors like Professor Anand Prakash and Prof.Tapan Basu, and to my friends like Prof.Malashri Lal, Prof.Sanjukta Dasgupta, Neelam

Saxena, Prof. Santosh Bakaya, Prof. Narinder Jit Kaur, Er. Ramendra Kumar, Dr. Anita Nahal, Prof. Anamika, Prof. Anisur Rehman, Prof. GJV Prasad, Prof. Kapil Kapoor, Prof. Raj Kumar, Prof. Lakshmi Kannan, Prof. Bratya Basu, Prof. Harish Narang, Prof.Harish Trivedi and many others—you have guided me with wisdom. I stand on the foundation of your teachings, humbled and grateful.

To my son Parthasarathi, the rhythm of my life--your quiet strength and unwavering love sustain me through every storm and stillness.

And finally, to Mr. Sankar Narayan Mallik – your elaborate reading of this manuscript, your deep love for its essence, and your keen eye for its nuances have been a gift. Your engagement was not just of the intellect but of the heart, and for that, I remain profoundly grateful.

May *Medusa* find a home in the minds and hearts of those who pursue her.

Nandini Sahu
www.nandinisahu.in

Contents

Medusa	17
Manthan—A Ghazal	20
A Cemetery of Dreams	22
An Extra Mile	24
An Ode to Every Woman	26
As the Going Gets Tough	29
Barefoot on Branched Grass	32
Boys Don't Cry	34
The Clay Lamp	36
Creative Liberty, a Tool of Polity	39
Culture Pickles	41
Embroidering a Love	43
Frozen in Time	45
Genie	47
God's Elect	49
Hurt People Hurt People	51
I Rhyme	53
Imago	54
Me, in Your Mirror	56
Medusa on Fire in Long Covert Dusks	58
Melancholia	63
My Sense of the World	66
Nature's Negotiation	69
Pulling Heart Strings	71
Revolting Illusory Penchants	74
Dushyant and Shakuntala	75
She Lives in Beauty	81
Sisterhood	83
Sonnet of the Taj	86
Sucking Silences and Solitudes	87
Tapoi	89
The Subliminal	91
The Unending Road	93
This Monsoon	95
Time is all We Have	97
Time Was All He Had	98
Time, the Relic	99
Waiting, in Synaesthesia	101
What My Mother doesn't Know	103
Women's Agency	104
Your Intimate Skies	105
The Difficult Daughter	107
Two Cities	110
A Country Called Love	113
Petrichor	115
Letter to My Unborn Daughter	116
The Akshyayapatra in Jagannath Puri	120

Medusa

I am Medusa, I merge with you,
my myriad-minded-molten-man,
the melic-moon-man.
See the sunny side of our youth and middle age
and let us amalgamate with our hearts beating each to each.

The melancholic sides of this mountain,
these time-teethed melodies,
the knowledge of the somber moments makes me amok-layered,
mist-mouthed. The mercurial mirror of my mind is in love's
melodious conch.

I am the Midas of the Muse. I germinate into a misty lunation.
You moan, "can you give me only one boon, my moony-moon?
Tell me in extenso. Will you be my blowtorch?"

Well, you know,
I will never reduce the illumination of my sparkling eyes.
Because you claim, my eyes have been your solitary gain
in the midst of life's never-ending pain.
Thus you make me some fitch.

In some birth, I was Medusa of the three Gorgons, daughter
of Phorcys and Ceto, sister of Graeae, Echidna, and Ladon --
the alarming and awe-inspiring beasts.
They predominantly did butch.

The gorgeous mortal, Medusa was the exemption in the family,
until she incurred the wrath of Athena, due to her conceit or
because of an ill-starred love affair with Poseidon-her
nocturnal notch.

This life, being Medusa,
I dance with the oceanic waves, move with the sea.
The rhythm of water has set my soul free. I get into my past
Surreptitiously, like getting into a cave.
My 'laugh of the Medusa' epoch!

I become two people in there, one says 'yes'
and one, 'no' to history.
Apparently, my beauty has surrounded you, encircled you,
left you gasping. Though you relish
my serenity even in that facade.

Just that, like a bad parent,
you planted a seed and walked away.
You did most definitely so, making me Medusa.
Now I have the courage
to let go of what I cannot change;
now I am life's firmest, wildest catch.

Medusa is non-judgmental, audacious,
beautiful, flexible yet unyielding.
Medusa is some myth and yet she is the ultimate truth.
Medusa is many lives in one life,
she can be like that veiled botch.

The flag and emblem of Sicily features on her head.
Two species of snakes contain her name: the venomous
pit viper Bothrops is Medusa and the nonvenomous sea serpent

Atractus is also Medusa.
She epitomizes philosophy, beauty and art.
She challenges the long tranquilized social slumber.
I clearly remember,
there is something beyond the fence of the past.

She is my chosen image of myself to show me
to an opaque world.
The range of her emotions are limitless. I am Medusa-myth,
I despise the doleful exclamation of some metal-faced ditch.

A very tentative person I have become, believing
in a benign God, the *Ardhanarishwar*. Singing like a free-swimming
carnal method of a coelenterate,
like a jellyfish is my free-thinking vouch.

I have an umbrella-shaped body
with cutting-edge tentacles on my couch.
Medusa is this phase of my life cycle
which substitutes with a monogamous phase.
I know, I should either write with my body
or choose to stay ensnared.

My '*écriture féminine*' takes encounters
with conformist patriarchal schemes.
I address this by the edifice of our robust
self-narratives and letterings.
You, my delectable, are with me in this scheme,
in my Medusa epoch.

God knows when your mild woman went wild, now that
the margin of your love has been rising from stretch to stretch.
You are the song of my ululating tongue.
Now life has become such.

Manthan — A Ghazal

Then you asked me, why do I shine so bright?
I said, my love, because I am your agenda of the light!

Then you pondered, how can my love be such a delight!
I said calmly, because love, at once, is opaque and clear daylight.

You brooded, "how can someone, how can someone
be a lover of your poise, your repute!!"

I said, *Samudra Manthan,* the churning of the ocean,
was accomplished to extract
the *Amrit*, celestial nectar,
where the Devas and the Danavas took part.

In a tug of war challenged to roil the elixir from the ocean
bed to attain immortality
and eternal life beyond bereavement.

The medieval Hindu Theology encompasses this legend
that the Devas were carrying the *am'it* away
from the Asuras, adamant.

Drops of nectar fell at four places
on the Earth-Haridwar, Prayaga (Prayagraj),
Trimbak (Nashik), and Ujjain, in their divine right.

In the churning of the ocean delightful treasures,
the archetypes
for their earthly and heavenly complements were brought.

Oceanic depths brought *Chandra*, the moon,
Parijata, the tree fragrant,
the four-tusked elephant *Airavata*, Lord Indra's mount.

Amid all that glory and glee of me,
your Lakshmi, you churned our fate,
using Mount Meru as the pole and Vasuki as rope,
the king of the serpent.

You became Lord Shiva,
you chose to devour the poison, you drank it.
In my *'manthan'*, you elected glory
for me and for yourself, venom was kept.

Nandini's conjecture--love churned me,
this love was my *'manthan'*.
Love took me out of the darkness of coalfields, like a granite.

Oh adorable! Love is ember, love granite,
love murky pebble, love- a shingle bright.
Love devotion, love renunciation, love meld,
love—a prayer from the heart.

A Cemetery of Dreams

A victim mentality is the ingenious clock of self betrayal. The character never develops. The story never ends—an infinite loop of personal hell. --J Mike Fields

Beneath a sky carved from stone,
where shadows bow over ancient bones—
your memories decay, whispering,
my prayers long silenced, deferred.
Here is the sand of what could have been,
catacombs of shattered reverie.
Each dream, a mourner once,
now concealed in the fragments of its own song.
A monument to grief stands silent,
hearts toughened into bitter gold.
The soil, once soft, now parched,
a famine of hope, no rain to quench.
The wind hums forgotten cries,
broken wings echo in the silence of the sky.
Paths lead only into endless night,
eyes that once dreamed, now blind.
A graveyard, vast and void of light—
each star refusing its flight.
The dawn, too afraid to rise,
fades behind brittle masks.
We walk on echoes, fragile,

in the endless dusk where sorrow drifts.
Dreams we carried have fallen asleep,
lost in shadows deeper than our grief.
And in this weeping silence,
there is beauty in the vast sweep
a cemetery sewn from longing,
where life, somehow, grows from tormented dreams.

An Extra Mile

Just as we were experiencing this peak of some bliss,
they showed us
how run-of-the-mill, how earsplitting,
defeating can be my terrain!
Anyway love, nothing matters now,
but this—throughout last night
I kept calling myself by your name.
And you responded to me by your term.

I called you my caballero in my admirable armor,
my cavalier, and
you broke the manacles of my forlorn agony.
I have been walking
this road for numerous years,
ephemeral in the curves in the shadow of my fears.
Yet, together, can we please gyrate and whirl,
with a blissful helix?

Today, I hold you intensely in my arms
as if there is no tomorrow.
Your smiles have been the antidote to all my sorrow.
No longer am I anxious of voyages on the roads of uncertainties.
Though you must show me the technique of dropping
my insecurities.

You talk of my compassionate antagonism, but I claim that
the uncertainty of a structured future is
rather so freeing! Still, I splurge in you, I grow up in you
in the midst of all that self-sabotage.

You taught me, the most important relationship
one has in life is with one's own self.
That is, with one's best version,
every single day. A high value woman that I am, knocking
on all the woods, I learnt to love
myself through censured condemnation.

Now, no longer me-and-you
but the promise of 'us' we articulate.
An uninterrupted journey, calm and composed,
is what we have designed.
But then these morning memoirs I must not disregard,
though I would love to walk an extra mile
intimate with you, contented.

An Ode to Every Woman

She bends to none, she is indomitable
that is the paradox of strength in her soft hands.
In lands unknown, she flourishes unseen,
through a vine that twines
through cracks of some ancient wall.
Silent footsteps, she grows,
rooted in soil she did not choose the source.

Her silence conquers you.
Her self is mirrored in the riddles told,
she spins her tales in sounds that loop and twist,
the echo mocks the fate that seeks her name—
she is both the actor and the stage's fervour.
In history's weave, she is the unseen thread
that holds together fabrics worn by kings.
She shapes the creation with shadows, yet she stands,
a quiet manufacturer of the future's frame,
while blazing bright within a hidden flame.

The cradle once a forge, where stars are cast,
her hands have tempered more than mortal dreams,
yet in her palms, the earth is fragile still.
She holds a universe in every drop of tear
a martyr's agonizing loss, a paradox of joy,
the sky is shattered with a single glance,
still she walks below its broken shards.

And in her breath, a tempest waits its time,
a storm contained in the gentlest breeze
Her quiet calm, the fiercest irony
her sisters call from distant points of light,
their voices tingle like coals beneath the sea.
Though the world may never see them rise,
they rise still, like the sun beneath the waves,
like a constellation shining in the dark
she moves as rivers carve their way through pebbles.
Unyielding, she bends to none but time.
The earth is etched beneath her steady limits.
each step a cipher, each breath an arcane
Tune woven through the loom of ancient skies—
in the hieroglyph, the cypher, the pictographs.

No servant to the whispered winds of men
she treads upon the fabric of the stars,
a silent navigator of the dark
a compass drawn from depths unseen, unknown,
the quill that inks her path is dipped in fire.

Her words are vessels, sailed on distant seas
where moonlight braids her hair with strands of gold.
In sacred halls, where echoes hide their shame

she dances the *tandav*, cloaked in shadows of the past,
yet radiant, she weaves her dawns in taffeta satin attire.

The womb, a forge, a kiln, where galaxies are born
her hands, the architects of tender dreams,
and yet, she wears her pain like ivory,
a mantle heavy, carved from ancient lore—
her crown is wrought from a noiseless, euphonic scar.
She knows, the same lesson will appear

in diverse forms until you pick up the grace
to respond inversely.

She is *Prakriti,* she does not rise, but rises still, a tree
whose roots drink deep of mystery's crimson rain,
whose branches scratch the edge of heaven's gate,
as thunder hails the coming of her reign.
The stars, her sisters, gather at her feet
their light, a silent deference to her might.

As the Going Gets Tough

We are like books. Most people only see our cover, the minority read only the introduction. Many people believe the critics. Few will know our content.---Emile Zola

The book of wisdom said, 'as the going gets tough,
the tough get going.'
I told, 'but I am brave!' And it said, 'how do you know?
Till today only delightful things happened to you,
you are young.'

I realized, justice builds a Chinese wall
between conflict and interest.
I pondered, is this calm a precursor of the storm?
Why is justice so unfair? The beginning of apocalypse, is it?

It talks to my truth—these changes in the anonymous, the cosmic.
One is system-position and
one people-position--I wonder, which
path to take? Then the bubbles burst with logic and magic.

Will the seed of this autonomy be equivalent to a greater success?
Are there some real prodigious people in the world,
unlike me, or
are there just larger challenges that
even the normal people can cross?

Tough people always don't roar.
They take a pause and try later.
The 'road, not taken' isn't elusive. Measuring the
immeasurable, immersive, they
merge with the boulevard immensely,
they selectively disappear.

I know that I belong to a restored world. And I am aware that
often superlative minds lose objectivity in pursuit of excellence.
Well, to win the game, you have to be a part of it first!

If you pull a rabbit out of box once, it's a miracle. If you do it
more than once, it becomes your habit.
Still, justice and kindness aren't
one and the same, but for a collaboration, one has to fight fit.

The life that we desire and the life that
we deserve aren't one and the same.
In the middle there is destiny indefatigable.
But the fact is, one has to
make a difference to the world and its unpredictable game.

Into a brave new world of possibilities
mind-numblingly I stride.
One failure is one step nearer to success.
Thus, even in my kitchen I serve
ladles of hope and love with a hint of asafetida,
it's such a delight!!

The shifting nature of power is—it exchanges hands.
Though time always doesn't reap inordinate things.
Every so often
tolerance is not a virtue but a freight, resonating the
cognizance it sharpens.

Sometimes we become more of exhibits than persons.
Then all liberties taken are quite deliberate.
Like a letter, sometimes destiny has to be picked
from where we left it last.

For tough people, a shadow has no wish of its own.
They suffer their memories and go where the road takes them.
No crown comes without a dagger—no matter how much
they mellow down.

Then they decide—go to a comrade's zone and
take a molten heart.
Be volatile. As Confucius agrees,
'Our greatest glory is not in never falling, but in
rising every time we fall.' That is the art.

Glitches are not stop signs; they are the stratagems of luck.
At the end of the rope, tie a tight knot and hang on.
Wait even if the very last key of the bunch opens the padlock.

Barefoot on Branched Grass

*Perhaps one did not want to be loved so much as
to be understood.* – George Orwell

There was no chronological precedence in making my story.
There was this layered conflict to worry.
I had been there and seen it all—devour someone
completely and spit them later—it was just so hallucinatory!

Yet I never believed in a life of dead ends.
There always was an open window constellatory.
Thus I have this annoying optimism to see a happy world
full of love and equilibrator.

The old antiquated thing called love. A beautiful mess
called love. Well, there were myths, but then, there were
truths as well. One foot in one foot out—analyzing more of life
than actually living it, more like a perfunctory.

I just needed to be rescued from there, the rug was
pulled out from under my feet. I thought, like Sartre—not choosing
anything, is still a choice! Barefoot on branched grass
life was nothing less nothing more than some compensatory.

I approached life like waves from the sea—one
after another, incessant, sporadic, never-ending.
Life lingered on me long after you loved me, every time.
Was it a manufactured façade, an interjectory?

I have been a copy of myself for too long,
massaging my own nerves.
Still I am this magnetic woman with golden eyes for you!
Loved by you, I get that strength. Loving you
back, I get great courage. you are my amelioratory.

After I had spoken breathlessly, you just smiled and said—*my
Goddess of words, don't tighten the strings of the Veena too much,
lest
it may break. Nor let it be so wobbly that it doesn't make any melody.
We are alive only when we love, let's live in this modest glory!*

Boys Don't Cry

Nature doesn't hurry, yet everything is accomplished --Lao Tse

'Boys don't cry,' they say,
as if masculinity were a fortress,
unshakable, armoured, a taciturn path.

But behind this myth lies a truth--
tears do not wear gender;
they are neither 'masculine'
nor 'feminine' and lenient, as their prerogative,
they are human,
breaking free from the chains of a designed faith.

Walls are assembled around the hearts,
young men are made to stand as sculptures,
silent, unyielding,
but effigies crack under time's pressure.
Emotion is not a flood to be dammed,
it is a river destined to flow—
gentle or intense, it must carve its path.
Metier is not silence,
not the suppression of grief
hidden behind clenched fists and bitten tongues.
It is the bravery in vulnerability,
to stand naked before the storm

and say, "I feel, and therefore I am."
Empathy blooms in the forgiving places
where the world tells you to be tough,
loud and clear.
In tears, there is a rebirth,
a release of the pain
that builds within the body
like implicit, unspoken words trapped
in a darkened chamber of ruth.

Men may cry not because they are feeble
but because they are alive
have loved
and lost,
and cared from the depth.

To cry is to resist,
to contest a legacy of silence
and replace it with tenderness
beyond just the home and hearth.
Let the tears flow like rain on droughted land.
Let them soak into the earth
nourishing the roots of a new empathetic path
that to cry is not hiatus
but to cultivate and nurture
a calm, predictable, divine life or death.

The Clay Lamp

> *I was never insane except on occasions when my heart was touched.* - Edgar Allan Poe

In the stillness of the Diwali night,
a clay lamp whispers light—
its flame, a breath, soft as silk,
born of earth and fire,
a fragile vessel of power that grow,
serene yet severe,
holding the universe within its glow.
It rests in the palm of the world,
humbled, moulded by hands
that know the secrets of time that flow.
A poet's prayer in clay,
its flicker a verse that dances
to the rhythm of wind and quietude.
Its flame is a heartbeat,
steady and strong,
yet tender as a lullaby.
Through this tiny flame,
the cosmos speaks in symbols—
a fire that does not scorch,
but purifies,
a warmth that does not sear,
but heals.

In its glow, the night is no longer dark
and the shadows bow,
retreating from the presence
of such quiet elegance, here and now.
The lamp is not merely clay
it is earth's breath,
transformed into light that may lie low.
It carries Diwali's piousness in its glow,
a beacon on a river of conviction, like the longbow.
Each flicker is an offering,
a prayer for the return of the sun,
a celebration of the triumph of light
over the dense armour of despair.
The lamp remains calm,
unhurried by the winds of time.
It knows its resolution—
to illuminate, then to fade,
not with sorrow, but with serene calm.
For the flame is not bound to the wick
it is the soul's fire,
free to leap, to float,
to merge with the river of souls departed with time
lighting the eternal night.
We have a choice
to hold the lamp,
and let it be put out in our grasp,
or to set it adrift
on the river's quiet arms,
releasing it into the flow
of something greater,
something vast and enduring.
In this humble clay lamp,
I find the power divine
in the festival of light and letting go.

Its glow retells
that even the smallest light
can break the deepest darkness
and in its tranquillity
I am complete again.

Creative Liberty, a Tool of Polity

In the territory of polyphony, intertextual voices collide,
creative liberty becomes the sovereign's disguise,
A crown made of metaphors, shiny but gloomy,
in the hands of the free, the heroic and the gullible.

Creative liberty, is it a weapon or a toy?
In the battle of minds, isn't it a polished decoy?
With colours and words, they carve out the lies
shape-shifting truth as illusion in camouflage.

In brushstrokes and verses, ideas sprout wings
but some call them birds, while others, mere strings.
A canvas so enormous, where thoughts goad to roam
yet somehow, each route leads back to the dominion.

Creative liberty, a sword made of air,
in the skirmish of ideas, watch out what's fair.
We wield it with elegance, though it's enveloped in chains,
free as a bird caught in imperceptible reins.

It's not just a dance, it's a delicate charade,
a revolution accomplished with paint and sparse bars.
The artist's heart tingles, ahh, how bright, how far?
Creative liberty, a light behind taverns.

From stage to screen, the script's set in shingle,
creative minds bloom, but never alone.
To question the law, to contest the throne,
creative liberty, the court's favourite pawn.

Artistic freedom, a weapon to wield?
Or feasibly just a looking glass, where veracity is concealed.
With words and colours, we profile and we twist
manufacturing the message that our champions defend.

Cheer for this choice so vast
in creativity's radiance, we dutifully cast.
In making a fire, or perhaps just a spark
creative liberty, an organized inventiveness in the murk.

Culture Pickles

The book of wisdom says, if you're ensnared,
caught in a pickle, trapped within a soup,
a quandary where no easy path is found.
From Dutch roots springs the word, 'pekel,' we say,
a brine of piquant taste, preserved in salt,
a jar of wisdom steeped in pane's bite.
The Pickle Jar, a theory of our time,
a vessel finite, like the hours we claim,
where moments, like the contents, must be filled—
the crucial first, the trivial must wait.
Each day, we pour in tasks both small and grand,
and time, once sealed, can never be returned.
Culture, that jar of knowledge, rich and vast,
contains the flavour of a people's soul—
their language, songs, beliefs, and works of art,
a myriad of voices, shared as one.
In that great jar, a pickle sharp and sweet
distils the essence of tradition's might.
From India's mango, spiced with turmeric bold,
to Korea's kimchi, fire caught in a jar,
each pickle tells a story of the land,
preserving the legacy in every bite.
The South's okra, crisp with dill and brine,
speaks of a way of life, of sun and soil.
In Europe, sauerkraut voices ages past,
while Eastern *achars* bridge old worlds with new.

In each preserved delight, a world resides,
a taste of history, a culture's conceit.
From one small jar, so many lives entwined—
a savoury link that joins the vast unknown.
Let me savour all that's held within,
for in these jars, a harmony does institute.
And art, like culture, spreads its wings and soars,
a canvas brushed by hands from distant shores.
Each stroke, a tale, each colour holds the past,
a living thread that weaves both old and new.
In every gallery, frames stand aligned,
whispering legacies the heart holds dear.
From marble, sculptors shape the dreams of men,
a monument to worlds both lost and found,
a dialogue between the young and old,
in stone and clay, in art, the stories live.
In calligraphy, the inked lines dance,
a poetry that flows,like a river eclectic.
And music, woven from the notes of time,
unites the hearts of those who dare to dream.
A collective language, sweet and pure,
that spans the gulf of culture and of creed.
Through art, through dance, through music, stories rise,
a vibrant thread that stretches across the skies.

Embroidering a Love

The wound is the place where light enters you. ---Rumi

Thus, asked me the weaverbird
the weaver of destiny.
How to embroider a love?
I pulled the heartstrings a bit, a bit more, that is.
The needle and the thread, apropos.

Embroidery's magic, in stories it holds,
with needles as wands, and colours as dreams.
It stitches together life's elaborate seams.
Glossy threads, like rivers that flow
Through fabric landscapes, they gently go,
Crafting beauty with every tiny stitch,
Like life's art, an intricate niche.
In the quiet of moments, fortitude required,
with nimble fingers to stitch a magnetism
love inspired.
Shapes emerge, like poetry in design
in every arch and twist, an untold tale is the sign.
From gentle emblems to patterns so fine
cross-stitch on the canvas, a timeless shrine
like relationships intricate and intertwine.
A weave of values, ethnicities and elegance
woven together in this delicate intergalactic.

A symbol of technique, patience and upkeep
embroidery whispers stories,like life.
In every chef-d'oeuvre, a portion of the heart
a feeling transcends like a cuisine of untainted art
bequests passed through the eons
a creation that appears.
In embroidery's embrace, stories reside
in every stitch, life's beauty is tied.
In too many irons in the fire, make room for love.
Cantankerous for the cause
it doesn't cloud lending with generosity
and pave way for Muse.

Frozen in Time

What cannot be said, will be wept ---Sappho

Since the day one,
we breathed in freedom,
we lived as individuals, together.
Your 'second home' became a place for you
more endearing, with a bit more scope.
The story was never about
what we got out of this love,
but about what we put into it.
Dreamers change the world, I had heard.
So I wondered,
How did it feel to have in life such certainty!
Because,
anything worth keeping
was certainly some anxiety!

My elemental emotions took
the best part of me,
and you had the flight of fancy
for me, the bride of escapade.
I felt home in myself
with your intense embraces
and my penmanship.
You filled a void that I never even knew that I had and thus,
I became your fantasy.

We lived happily ever after, ahead by a century,
with a noble emotional inevitable quest.
We got lost in the pinnacle shyness
of the canopy of foliage. Life was
carefully planned and diligently executed thus.

And then, as the table turned,
frozen in time, I want to deal with you
now,
fair and square.
Life is in a ticking clock.
Love is malleable, moot,
you don't like being you, any further.

When you can't push people away,
you drive them away
and you do so when you know
the only thing more dangerous
than being tough-headed is
being soft.
So you 'settle' for a permissible matter
instead of a love that's devout.

Well, yes! Only mud *settles,* isn't it?
I know that only I'm the keeper of the key
to your heart.
The quest for perpetual happiness is illogical, unjust.
You will understand this if you
step into the shoes of my life,
now that we both are hugging the porcupine.
I look in your eyes and smile just as
'home-wrecker' is added to the list of adjectives here.
After all,
pain builds one's character!

Genie

When we are tired, we are attacked by ideas we conquered long ago.
                              ---Frederich Nietzsche

I stepped into your ocean,
seeking restoration,
like rivers returning to their source.
The currents of your love
swept me back to where I began,
and you to your own shores.
I can't shake the feeling
that I've been a guest in your heart,
though you gave me the sea.
I drank it down,
like love that's never mine to claim,
love that barely touches the seaboard.
Today, you know that you spent half your life
moulding your light on me.
Now it's my turn to shine.
But deep down, I know
no matter how hard some of us polish our lamps,
the genie never appears.
Sealed inside a bottle, the genie waits for
a force of untamed magic
with the power to change worlds.
Unencumbered by a wish,
it rises, smoke swirling,

eyes gleaming with ancient knowing.
'Three wishes, my Master,' it says,
'but be wise, for desire can twist and turn.'
In the territory of wants and dreams
every wish comes with a price.
Greed is a trap,
listen to your heart's quiet call,
the genie's gift is both benediction and expletive,
and in chasing dreams, we lose our way.
In the end, it returns to its bottle,
waiting,
for the next soul to release its control.
A genie's tale is one of longing,
and in every wish, magic lies hidden.
As you shape your dreams,
let wisdom be the chaperon,
for even in the heart of desire,
it's compassion
that plays the illumination.

God's Elect

Observe the wonders as they occur around you. Don't claim them.
Feel the artistry moving though and be silent. ---Rumi

She is fractured yet complete
a paradox of past and present
a transformed woman
wrapped in the same skin
carrying the jagged edges of someone else's angst.
Her mind, a mirror that never forgets,
reflects the pain of another's sleuth
like an echo
that lingers long after the sound dwindles.
Silver tongued
all at once sharp and soft
cutting through silence
with words both noxious and sweet
she is Medusa, she is God's elect.

A paradox she wears like armour
in the quiet corners of credence
where hearts reach out but rarely touch,
there is a whisper about her:
she is God's chosen.
But chosen for what?
A crown of grace or a burden of spikes?

They walk with flames in their hearts,
fire that freezes them in their tracks,
moving toward a light that blinds
somehow illuminates the path
of their steps that are heavy
yet weightless with faith,
a cosmic dance that defies enormity.
Threads of destiny weave through her life
disparaging and delicate
binding her to a love that suffocates
and yet sets her free.
In her replication the world is
tangled in some contradictions
chosen and forsaken
loved and unloved in the same breath.

Hurt People Hurt People

Where does a thought go when it's forgotten? **-Sigmund Freud**

There's a bruise deep inside,
a scar invisible. Itched into the mind,
it throbs beneath the surface of every word they say.
They carry wounds like burdens,
old wounds that never healed,
memories that festered,
shadows of what there was no proclamation.
Sometimes their words are stilettos
cutting not because they want to,
but because they can't help it
as though the only way to speak
is to bleed
through the language they cultured.
In their eyes, see now a storm, and now calm,
now rage, now muddle,
a swirling mix of fear and self-righteousness.
Love and trust
are fragile, perilous.
They don't know they're hurting people
to them, it feels like fortification,
a shield against the pain
they expect from the world,
preparing for wounds
even before they arrive.

Hurt people build walls,
fortresses of sharp words and distant glances,
and sometimes, without knowing,
they turn into the very thing they fear,
passing on their pain like a gratified inheritance.
There's a maze of memories
a labyrinth of sorrow
where every path leads back to the same place—
the place where they were hurt
and the echo of that moment
never really fades.
They hurt because they want to survive,
and in that survival, subsistence
they forget the texture of hurt
that others can feel it too
and the baton will be passed on!

I Rhyme

I rhyme with the rhythm of roots deep-buried
earth-hum thick in the sap-streaked veins,
green symphony, tree-thrum, pulse in the hollow
leaf-chatter caught in the wind's wild strain.
I rhyme with the beat of the drum-beat tapping
fingers on frets and the bowstring's draw,
sound unfurling like vines from the soil,
a song with no end, but yes! no need for more.
Ah, the music of voices, the rise of the chorus,
language spun round the notes' sharp turns,
word-stitches sewn into time's slow march
and verse where the rhythm of nature tingles.
I rhyme with the moss and the melody rising,
footfall soft on the forest's floor
where poetry swells in the sweep of branches,
and life plays its chord ceaseless.

Imago

A writer is a world trapped inside a person. -**Victor Hugo**

It is an unconscious idealized mental image
a cerebral zone
of someone
which follows me daylong.
There is a face I've never truly seen
etched in soft shadow, glowing behind my eyelids
when I turn from the light.
This face is not a person,
but a summary, like a rough draft,
ongoing, floating like a silent prayer
I have been whispering my whole life
without any such eloquence of the arguments
with myself.
It wears fragments of someone I once needed
a voice, a hand reaching out to me,
the slope of a smile caught in the static of memory.
Yet it changes, shifts its weight
like clouds thickening into shapes
I think I recognize
until they vanish again.
My worst battle is between
what I know and what I feel.

I have followed this imago
ingenuous, naïve.
With every decision to track it
as if my steps are tracing an orbit around
an invisible star.
It draws me close, then fades
into the periphery of my days
into the edges of dreams
where the colours run wild on the canvas.
Sometimes, I wonder who gave me this,
this ghost of a guide,
this half-formed vision of love
etched with longing I never chose
but wear like an old coat
that still fits.
Did someone give it to me,
or did I pull it from the stories I made of myself
long ago?
Before I knew how people fail
before I understood that even love
is not enough to save me.
I carry this face like the national flag
On Independence Day
hoping one day to meet it
unabridged.
To see it standing before me
no longer a dream,
but flesh and bone,
someone who can finally
reach back
with assurance and aplomb.

Me, in Your Mirror

Between what is said and not meant and what is meant and not said, most of love is lost. **-Khalil Gibran**

They always said, *you have a beautiful smile!*
And you said, "you are beautiful, with a
stunning smile. Not lopsided, never sarcastic,
open-ended, inclusive, comprehensive, never fading smile.
Your smile begins and ends in the
middle, in the center of your opulent, jovial lips!"

That kept me pondering—*does anyone essentially
define a smile this way?* That is when I saw
myself in your mirror!

I take time, all the time in the world, to smile for you,
because it's the harmony of my soul. It's the music
that you composed.
I know, my smile is contagious, you catch
it like flu. And now my smile travels around the world
through your lips.

If you feel my smile in your stomach
and if you feel butterflies in there
don't leave it concealed.
Start an epidemic swift, get the world infested by us.

Let them reminisce our infectious smiles.
We are born to love, that is our essence.

Well, you are the secret hiding place
of my smiles. You are my home.
You smile at me, I smile back.
Thus one smile makes two.
When I smile, you beam
with a dense desire to reconnoiter.
You explore my depths, you fill my contours
you leave me with deeper longing and amatory wish.

We are caught up in this whirlwind, coveting never to look back.
I smile and create a language of intimate collaborations.
My smiles send an instant message to you-- let me melt in
your arms.
And then the world smiles with us in tandem.
We merge, we *drink to the lees.*
In your benign arms my world belongs.

Medusa on Fire in Long Covert Dusks

These Medusa-mellow-moods.
Ah, these!

I have been that fiery ace beyond
your remotest dreams.
My five feet four inches mount is a boiling desert
of sand dunes, mirages and retreat,
the only relief
from which has been
to be in the dusks of our
consummation, deep and intimate.

My eyes are sweltering, like comets
which can char anyone's mind
and scale the temperament.
My mouth is a volcano and my kiss,
a detonation, an ignition.
My embrace is a ring of fire
and my breath is the brutal blast
of sunny gust.
My tress is like some intense flicker
and each string of hair on me
is a discrete catalyst.
My hidden depth is a subterranean contour

like a foaming sacrificial fire
in which you scorch and melt.
But then my love, every time,
every time you
come out pure and even more expectant.

You put your points
across—on corporeal desire –
you bring those to the table;
but then you moan, *nothing kills the pleasure
of erotica than this complimentary cypher.*
I think, there is something egalitarian in here,
because
longing between us is like a binary death,
like some instant dying of our blended breath
or like vanishing of an unfamiliar bizarre perfume
flowing between us swiftly
in this naked compartment.
But today, I felt, nay, I am rather sure,
this chamber is seared and singed like amber.

The deeply private person that I am,
I do not know who knows
our depraved surreptitious truth.
I do not see who parks itself astride my back
who grazes my sides so tenderly
on my way to the shadowy elevation.
But still, I am so glad,
you express yourself in your element.

All my body is sugar to your mouth
and all my fragrances, grassland to your senses.
Our positions keep changing
like locations of a prime-mover

on this large queen-size bed--our pulverized den.
Our inner voices echoing each-to-each
and parts of the body speaking
silently, having a dialogue as much.
My ears are scarlet with your favorite
game of biting my nape and earlobes
while I am in concert with your
masculine body hair to
your midriff to tailbone to
fingertips to toe-nails.
You whisper, the art of unclothing
is also a sculpture one must master as such.
The perfect foreplay, the act of arousal,
is more like the Bildungsroman on your part.
It's the science of peeling the skin of
love, erotic love, that is.
Covered underneath is
some feebleness, fragility of roguish arch.
Eyes play their part in tandem with our bodies,
deeply probing into each other
in this surreal, transcendental trance
we merge, we march.
I feel my body feather soft and cotton light
my sentient gets fragrant
in your elevating love-making act.
In your strong masculine embrace
I melt bit by bit, beyond the debauch.
You sing a divine song
into my being.
I become yours.
After all, I master the art of submission
and that of comprehensive surrender.

Now, I clasp your elongated lithe arms
and fierier hands
than fire. I love the quavering margins of our bodies
and each string of our hair redolent of longing.
The lively fleeting feet, the fine agile thighs
the rounded supple breasts
and scintillating eyelids craving
the long clandestine dusks,
our twisted weapons,
breast to breast in the loom—
that's the attitude of the moment.
The faded red lamp, blooming
with magical shadows
and its overcast objective gear
kindle a wizard flame.

It always happens with us, your body
does this rendezvous with mine —
fond, subtle terpsichore twirling.
The animate, insatiate globule of my nipples
in your mouth — you touching me, secure,
shielding, penetrating, your
robust tongue and strong fingers
finishing where I had been waiting
for years
in the jasmine-slimy-cave—
I moan and sigh!
A little teary too.
Yes, it happens.

And here you are sitting alongside,
legs to one side, convulsion in the body.
I can bear it no longer.
I touch the privileged part

of your banana-trunk-like thighs.
Your response is to interchange.
Then there is this shudder.
My neck and nape are numb.
My heart wallops and soars
as my fingers go to your glide
and guide you *there* to the hidden treasure.

"Come slowly, love!" I fumble.
But nay! After making Medusa a poem-poem,
it's time for you to twirl.
Now you are noncompliant, defiant.
It's no less than some divine accomplishment.
You are arrhythmic,
like that gush of wild west wind!

Melancholia

If you are too tired to speak, sit next to me for I too, am fluent in silence. **-R Arnold**

It drifts like fog through the open window
soft as a whisper
but heavy as stone.
A shadow that wraps itself around me,
slowly, like the sky swallowing the sun.
It seeps in, like water through cracks,
filling the spaces you didn't know were hollow.
A river in your chest, quiet, relentless,
drowning every spark, until all you know is cold.
In the parsimony of shade
this pirouette of the weeping willow
It's hard to say goodbye to someone
who you never met
but who existed in the air you breathed.
A cloying tale. That almost happened,
just about happened, but it didn't.
The thrill of the chase now
is not the chill of the catch.
That is *melancholia*.

It feels like a clock ticking in reverse,
each second pulling me further from me,
as if time is a tide dragging me
to a bottomless sea.
I am becoming a tree in autumn,
bare branches reaching towards ancient history
written on the lines of my palm
the lines that resemble
leaves falling like memories
broken promises, lost moments,
dispersed in the wind.
After all, the heart is a mirror,
reflecting only what's gone,
a hollow drum echoing
with the rhythm of what I no longer am.
I wear melancholia like a second skin,
tight, suffocating,
yet familiar,
and yet I master the art of smiles.
What a thing to say!
Melancholy and smiles like hands in gloves.
It's a room with no windows,
a storm with no rain,
just the ache of thunder rolling
slow, endless, like a song that never finds its
concluding stanza.
Penultimate is the only fate.
I wonder
if I am the sky
and if the blue is a mask
and beneath it all
I am the only cloud
drifting, empty,
always on the verge of breaking.

The poetics of melancholia
As life's presence in my city has thinned
the city has grown bereft.

I've a heart murmur with a condition.
I know the distinction
between fairness and vengeance.
Life may not fix it, but life must concede it.

My Sense of the World

You cannot swim for new horizons until you have courage to lose sight of the shore. -**William Faulkner**

In my world, laughter rises early
like birdsong calling in the light,
steady and untiring, it spreads,
wakes voices softened by sleep and dreams.

Here, neighbours speak with open faces,
even strangers nod, their gaze warm,
as if kindness, no longer rare,
is just breath we share.
Roots reach and bind the earth as we walk
trees bending in generous shelter,
air sweetened by gardens where people dig
shoulder to shoulder, soil and sweat alike,
hands growing calloused, but soft to hold.

This world makes room for soft hearts
for quiet times and unhurried days
for conversations that need no rush
eyes meeting in real, human time
giving moments the space to breathe.

I plant what I hope will thrive
fruit trees in empty lots
flowers in vacant windows
words that nurture or heal
small acts that ripple beyond me
one good thing feeding another.
To me, each step substances, each hand counts,
not a single gentleness goes unnoticed.

I know that it's the water inside the ship
That drowns it, not the water around it.
A perfect relationship is nothing
but the chimera of the mind.
Thus, I have a slow burning will of my own
like the moon.

I build optimisms with the parts of me
that still remember grace.
I am strong, deep like the blue
and am beautifully complex.
I am a beautiful ruin, beautiful because of
all that I have been through.
One door opens for me when one closes,
and I see diamonds in the dust of the past.
In the cracks in my heart, I let
lights in.
I am actually living
in the lost pieces of myself.
Now I am like a nail—waiting for a hammer,
 holding my breath.
These are my diluted pleasures.
I am learning to live with it,
finding new ways of coping.
An audit of the heart is the need of the hour,

my sense of the world
Is the new world-order--
what/who is the 'constant'?
Do I inherit
the *wasteland?*

Nature's Negotiation

If I had a flower for every time I thought of you, I could walk through my garden forever. ---Afred Lord Tennyson

I hadn't thought of writing
about nature's negotiation until you told me
what stone we are carved from,
what lesions make you, you,
and me, me, to this extent.

The nights of solitude wound me,
the yellow moon incites my scars.
Yet, I am consumed
by the melancholy of your extant;
my past suffers in its bereavement.

You fleece the things that you should share
and say what I want you to hide.
I pretend to laugh.
But my ebullient laughter can't hide my scars.
I can't put my quiet ache under
this disguise at this moment.

You have come to my retreat after long yearning
you have given words to my yearnings.
Isn't this negotiation of nature enough
for us my love?
Isn't our home
home-enough? Our nights, night enough?
Aren't oceans, ocean enough, butterflies,
butterfly enough,
rains, sunsets, mountains, birds, wind,
sunrise, leaves, ladybugs
enough in their nature and spirit?

Nature took off its life
from the day of our acclimatization.
Now, I see an icier shoulder
on the negotiation table.
I see a responsive flora and not too wearisome a boulder,
and our dropping of chains for shackles—
well, I comprehend no other floor of commitment.

Pulling Heart Strings

A man must first find himself before he finds his woman.
Otherwise, he will continuously damage every woman he comes in
contact with along the way. (anonymous)

Making you the resolution of life, I am clueless now
about my own sense of the word 'purpose'.
If I think anything at all,
the thoughts are just on matters of the heart.

Isn't it fascinating to paradigm the character of a woman
who has no life beyond? The theme of this song is—
I have presented my life to you.
Presenting the elemental woman

to the man who is he-knows-what-he-is! Though
this must be 'normal' in some world elsewhere.
'Me' in this story
is a missing female character on days
of your choice—given subjectivity.

I disappear without a trace, you see!
Of late I am too interested in missing characters.
I find myself as in a soliloquy, talking aloud to myself!

*"Look! Look at yourself looking at Whatsapp, social media and
at that house-dress he left in your wardrobe, and his half-finished Beer
in your portico, and look at the right side of your bed!*

*Look at the plates he likes to eat in or the glasses he likes to drink in.
Look at your slightly swollen undereye and the nose-pin or
the dot on your forehead. Look how some lives are a prolonged sinch!*

*On missing-days, look how you experiment with left-over food
from the refrigerator and with ill-fitting fabrics.
Look how he prefers one disagreeable over another disagreeable.*

*Look at your enviable profession, the fine books that you yield,
and your manicured neat hands, remembering some other obnoxious.
Look how freakily free he is, living multiple lives!*

*Look how he is having two strong legs and yet a Merman's tail too—
he is actually having it all!"*
Except that I pretend unhappy, but am content
and you are not, yet you envisage to be gratified.

You have given me a critique of seclusion, this is melancholy
rather than depression. Sadness rather than despair.
I no more weep alone in the kitchen on missing-days

and no longer put up a social face.
I make-believe to be baffled by the many lovers
who come and go through this revolving door.

I tell myself--- *I have to be likeable;* well, I am exceptionally
accomplished at it!
I, thus, am incredibly liked by one and all. I apologize
my unrequited lovers for my want of wanting them convenient.

But this is another life, like exactly what I want.
Carrying the old playhouse inside me
all my life, very heavy though, I am willing now to let it go.

Nay, let me stop here. What is the point of
writing a poem that makes one chuckle and shed a tear or two!
What is the need to make heartstrings on hand! *"Look, change the mood!"*

I have been very taken with this *Jasmine Itr*, its erotic fragrance,
a bit of warm and harsh. I look at the narcissism of love
pulling my heartstrings way too hard; now I want to be extinct.

Revolting Illusory Penchants

There are no facts, but only interpretations.
        - **Frederick Nietzsche**

In the silent realm where shadows loom
a spectre rises
from the unseen depths
an illusion of wrongs, wearing masks of truth
in the theatre of thought
the ballets in whispers.
It lingers in sleepless nights, a flicker in dreams
a twisted echo of perception
where the line between reality
and fiction blurs
distorting the shapes of what we know.
This fog of injustice
there lies a spark, a flame kindled by empathy,
a reflection of real grievances
a mirror to the world's wounds, unseen, unhealed.
Even in illusion, there's a cry,
a plea for compassion, to hold, to understand,
to see beyond the veil of minds,
and let love bridge the distance,
real or otherwise.
In these whispers of injustice
heed the call
and through this fog
find the keys to liberate hearts.

Dushyant and Shakuntala

(I. The Meeting in the Grove)

In primeval forests where rivers sang
beneath the shadow of sacred trees
there bloomed exquisiteness, untouched, unseen,
the daughter of sage and forest's queen.
Shakuntala, fair as the *Faerie Queene,*
her spirit interlaced with nature's might.
Dushyant, a combatant sovereign
hunting in the woods, heard nature's intone.
Drawn by the grove's enchanting spell
he found the maiden where blossoms fell.
She stood by the streams, shy as the breeze,
a nymph in the shades of banyan trees.
Eyes met, time stood still, love at first sight,
hearts enthused by love's primeval joy.
Under the gaze of watching skies,
they pledged their betrothal with whispered sighs,
and there in nature's verdant womb,
their love did bloom, unfold.
He came armoured with the pulse of conquest
crowned by valour, hunting alone
seeking beasts in the depth of the forest
yet there, he found her, the unknown.
Shakuntala, raised by the whispers of leaves
by creatures immaculate in their names.

Her skin was clay and earth, her spirit fire
her heart unclaimed by kings or contests.
But what is a woman left to fate
to a king who drops and moves on?
She's the vine wound tight around the gate,
elapsed once the sweep is gone.

(II. The Ring and the Parting)

Stay with me, she moaned low,
now duty called, he had to go.
With quivering hands, he gave a ring,
a token destined to memory's string.
Hold fast to this, he softly said,
and in my heart, you're never dead.
He left, the king with a paramour's pain,
to rule his land, though love remained.
But fate, it seems, had other negotiations,
and soon would play its astute hands.
Did he love her, or did he love the grove
the thrill of a bond without the crown's weight?
What is love when love must rove
answering always to the call of fate?
He leaves her a ring, a loop of vows
yet departs with hands free of chains.
For he wears the crown, unbroken, unsawed
while she waits, bound by love's remains.
For him, love is a respite, a balm
a dalliance, a drift in the forest's calm.
For her, it's a mantle, a path unchosen,
a root in the earth, eternal, frozen.

(III. The Curse of the Sage)

Suns turned to moons and seasons passed
till that day, with her heart steadfast
she journeyed forth, to palace grand
with love and hope in quaking hand.
Yet in the grove, a curse took shape
a sage's wrath, her fate's dark cape.
Since you failed to heed my call,
your love shall fade, forgotten as trivial!
With words of scorn and fire
he cursed her heart's dear desire.
The king forgot his woodland bride
as clouds cloak stars in deepest night.
The ring, lost in river's stream,
severed Shakuntala's enduring dream.
In the depths of the grove, a curse took root
scorned love, an old man's rage.
Why does it fall on her, silent, mute,
the delusion of a lover's mirage?
He forgets her, as kings disremember wars,
as hunters leave prey unseen.
But curses are roots, they run deep, they stay
and love is shadowed by what has been.

(IV. The Years of Parting)

Alone moseyed the ecofeminist, bearing his child
in lands feral and forests wild.
Rivers vibrant and mountains steep
she prayed to destiny in slumber deep.
For ages, she roamed with mourning's weight,
yet held to hope despite her fate.
The son she bore, prince Bharat,

ordained to rule the lands far and wide.
With lion's strength and eagle's gaze
he grew, unscathed by sorrow's haze.

(V. A Woman in Waiting)

She groomed his son through forests eclectic,
while he sat contented on his jewelled seat.
Where is justice when men resolve fate
while women wait in shadow's heat?
Masculine honour, the privilege of kings,
sways like branches that break and bend;
yet always lands where the hawk takes wing
leaving the earth for the earth itself to mend.
And still, she waited—a daughter of dust,
for a crown's return, for a ring's faint glow.
For a woman waits, as if in trust,
while kings move on, as men must go.

(VI. The Recognition and Reunion)

In royal halls, the king that day
beheld a boy in forest's sway
strong and fierce, with spirit bright
a mirror image of himself in might.
And soon, with memories returned,
his heart aflame with love that burned.
They met, as fate decreed
by love and memory freed.
In her eyes, the dawn's mist and light,
in his gaze, the star of night.
Shakuntala stood, a shadow unknown
her love intact, though sorrow-worn.
The ring restored, the curse undone

and fate at last its full course run.
When they met again, fate was the crown,
destiny unlocked herself with the wedding
ring returned to Dushyant by the fisherman.
Dushyant claimed his blood, as kings lay claim
to the earth and the sea's untouched charms.

In her heart, it held the memory's truth,
a grove still shadowed by broken dreams.
And though she was queen, her spirit knew
what love was, unspoken, beneath the seams.
For love in a forest is root and thorn,
bound to earth, yet free, forlorn.
But love in a palace is chiselled stone
a thing of the heart, yet carved alone.

(VII. Epilogue)

Their love is a story to be told
through fire-lit nights, in voices intrepid.
Of love that bloomed in forest's shade
and by curse and memory reversed
yet destined by gods' decree
to birth a line of royalty.
She returned, a queen, but knew too well
what it meant to live as a myth, anonymous.
For history calls it a tale of love
while she is the song in a muted tongue.
In a world of authority, power may move free
between groves and thrones
while love bears its hampered tree.
Thus lives the tale, in shadows cast,
of Dushyant's love, too brief to last.

In myth and folklore lives the tale, forever sung
as long as stars in heaven are hung
the story of love, both Spartan and embellished
of Shakuntala's portrayal intrepid.

She Lives in Beauty

She steps lightly, she treads softly
carefully choosing not to distract the morning sun;
her voice, a gentle breeze
that carries compassion in each syllable.

Her floral dresses swaying like a garden in bloom,
each one a quiet celebration
of softness, of grace, that is her garmented metaphor,
that is her panoramic world petal by petal.

Her warmth makes the day unfold
with the ease of summer-rain, drenching us in light.
She lives in beauty, her smile—
an echo of the eternal.

Empathy in her eyes, like the stillness of dawn,
where wisdom does not bellow, but listens unwearyingly,
offering a hand, a dialogue,
a heart large enough to hold us all.

The quiet flowering of a soul in full bloom
like a breeze through the open windows,
like an ode to the rivers blue, she flows with the
dappled brushes. In her elegance, mesmerised we are.

We live in her beauty, she paints warmth in the air,
and in its gentle glow, like a lullaby sung to the seas
through tangled thoughts and humming bees;
her presence, even her silence, is a moral of sophistication.

Her molten heart can cradle a fragile bud;
she reminds us that to be wise is to be tender.
Lifting our burdens we never knew we carried,
she does our hearts unfurl and heal.

Calm like the moon's soft sigh,
she flows as the west wind beneath a velvet sky.
Her insights ripple, spreading wide,
a stream of warmth, in me does she confide.

Like water carving through earth's core,
she silhouettes with grace, forevermore.
Her touch, a balm, her words, a song,
in her world of beauty, we all belong.

And as she winds through time and space
her valediction leaves behind a soft embrace,
memories for a lifetime, a path of peace, a radiant gleam,
like streams flowing through a dream.

Sisterhood

> *"Women instinctually know how to nourish each other,
> and just being with each other is restorative."* - **Tanja Taaljard**

Thus, I talk a lot about solidarity and sisterhood.
My sisters and archetypal sisters may please hear me out!
I have been accessible yet peripheral,
non-judgmental, non-indulgent
beyond all glamour, glory and the social scanners
getting into reckless and pointless things yet.

I fancy my sisters to appreciate, in spirit,
that I live alone in the company of others living alone,
each one fortified by a lone ache of the heart.

The fact that I was born in July,
the volatile time of the year—
they need not categorize any much of my temperament.

Now there are mornings when I wake up but
I don't like to get up. Lying on the bed,
I regret my squandered years that I have been that type
who fits in anywhere. Ahh, why I have been just so perfect!

Full of campaign and stratagem, I still believe that
it's possible to change the world, this planet.

My sculpted sisters often look at me and sigh,
'I want to be a woman like you, bold and independent.'

Dear sisters, I am that imperfectly-perfect-woman,
take me as I am, maybe with a pinch of salt?
I wish you saw some tiresome apprehension in there.
Some enduring experiences utmost.

Why only sisters? Even my mother's isolation
is getting into my nerves. It's a detrimental amalgam.
Some kind of panic of an avoidable alarm, some fright.

Yet, the gulf between me and my 'sisters' has told me,
seclusion has its own goodies to offer --I cheer up myself,
which some of them make-believe not to make out.
Solitude has become my only discipline,
my skill, my dexterity and my mental state.

These days I live in a new home, a newly
constructed house, that is, where no one lived in the past,
no one made love, no one died
nor none got exhausted. Just that,
the highlighted nature of the house makes it look
paradoxically alive and animate.
It has a romantic, quixotic tonal quality, that is.
And I call it, 'the power of white!'

Here, in fact, yet elsewhere, I sleep poorly,
for forever I am sleep disoriented.
I boast I swank that I take its advantage, to become
so prominent and, well, such distinguished!

I have heard that the female combatant
knows how to fight with the world even without a contest.

She discerns when not to raise her sword,
but as a substitute she holds up her heart.

A sister's safeguard is not a resistance
to counter others, but a sanctuary for a wretched heart.
If recuperative of each other is the case with sisterhood,
someone please refurbish, revamp me, be my
special kind of mind-and-body-double,
no matter where and what.

Sonnet of the Taj

Beneath the moon, a marble dream ascends
a palace carved from sorrow's silent stone
its ivory towers, where love's whisper bends
stand testament to grief's eternal throne.
Here, Shahjahan's heart beats in crypts of coldest white
a queen entombed, her daintiness still aglow.
The Taj, a monument to interminable night
where roses bloom, though time has turned to snow.
Each dome a sigh, each arch a lover's plea
the pinnacles stretch like hands that touch the sky.
This tomb, a kingdom where the heart is a marble sundry
a fortress erected so love would never die.
In every stone, a promise lies engraved
love outlives death and then time incarcerated.

Sucking Silences and Solitudes

Sucking the architecture of silence
I stand in room of curated emptiness
where silence is built into the walls,
a history in pauses
browse, scroll.
In a world of mirrored faces
where each silence echoes, edited, rephrased
and each solitude is a script, uploaded
what is real? What is missing?
Solitude is so digital, stitched by code
and pixels of people we may never see,
a diaspora, spread thin by a thousand clicks,
a culture of the re-imagined, re-posted.
In the hush of this networked reality
truths are braided with images
each story double-clicked, re-storied, unlinked
memories are hyperlinks, silences, 404.
Colonized by feeds and filters
the geography of self rewritten in fonts,
where silence feels strange, uncanny
an absence I try to fill with noise.
This solitude—exported, translatable,
an artifact buried in timelines,
unrooted, adrift from its origin—
can I reclaim it, rewrite it in the language
of something real?

In the architecture of my silence,
I wear my screens like masks
voices layered and distilled
until all that's left is an echo,
a solitary vibration, whispering back,
where are you in all this noise?
Solitude is scattered across servers
silences—exported, unmoored.
How do I find the ground again
the real, the blood, the skin?
In a world where data dreams in shadows
and solitude speaks only in borrowed words,
I seek an empty room
to sit still, to listen to silence
as it breathes, as it hums, as it returns
something untouched,
disparate, unknown.

Tapoi

In primeval maritime Utkal, the seas did a clarion call,
the merchants sailed on winds to aloof lands
to Java, Sumatra, Bali's golden sands,
to Sri Lanka, where palm trees touch the sky,
and to Madagascar, where the wild waves cry.
They filled their ships with treasures bright and rare
returning rich, with fortunes meant to share.
Among them was a merchant, noble, grand
his daughter, Tapoi, bloomed like flowers of sand.
Her hair like cascades in the night and eyes held the stars,
her brothers cherished her, she was apple of their eyes.
But one day, Tapoi's heart, a flame of gold,
desired the moon—a treasure to behold.
She asked her father, rich beyond compare,
for a golden moon to match her beauty rare.
The goldsmith's hands began their patient toil,
shaping moonlight from the earth's bright spoil.
Yet fate, with cruel hands, did intervene
her father died before the moon was seen.
Her mother, too, was taken away by the fates,
as the moon was forged, shining from heaven's gates.
Her brothers, strong as oak, with hearts of steel,
set sail upon the seas to trade and deal.
They left their sister in the wives' cold care,
who, in their envy, whispered cruel despair.
Her wish for gold has brought us grief and pain,

they murmured, weaving tales like storms of rain.
They cast her out, her gentle heart oppressed,
and sent her wandering in the wilderness's breast.
When the brothers returned from distant shores,
with wealth and spices, riches in their stores,
they found their sister, broken, lost and torn
a flower trampled by the winds of scorn.
In rage, they punished their wives who dared betray
their comely sister in such forbidding a way.
They brought her back from shadowed woods of night,
restored her to home to her heart's delight.
And in due course, a marriage rich was made,
a merchant's lad her fortune did persuade.
Tapoi's tale, like seas that rise and fall,
lives on in Utkal's folk songs, reminisced by all.
Through her grief, a lesson still does flow
that wealth and love are tides, they just come and go.
In the golden sails of Utkal's past,
Tapoi Myth, like the *Cinderella Folktales* of France,
are celebrated as the ocean's mellifluous songs.

....

PS.: The Tapoi myth is a traditional Odia story from the rich maritime history of Odisha about a woman who prays to Goddess Mangala to get her brothers back and avenge her suffering. Tapoi is treated poorly and waits for her brothers to return, but is only supported by her youngest sister-in-law. While wandering, she sees girls worshipping Goddess Mangala and prays to her for help. Tapoi offers "Khuda" (broken rice) to the goddess and promises to fast on Sundays. Her prayers are answered and her brothers return. The brothers dress Tapoi up as a goddess and send her to the ship to meet their wives. To avenge her suffering, Tapoi cuts off the noses of all the wives except the youngest.

The Subliminal

I always pick the right side
even if I am the only one standing there.
Because
when tall men cast short shadows, I understand
that
the sun is on the top of our head.

In this inimitable love story
we had always been on borrowed times,
like today, on this subliminal day and date.
A purist that I have been,
I believe in codependency
though you may think it's not to-be-ought.

There's plenty of fish in the sea
but I have been afraid of water.
Is it some sort of subconscious resentment?
Or I am grossed out of all of it?
You have been slipping through my fingers
some days. That is it.
But I wish I could fix the picture and not let it slip away
from our eternal presence of the past.

The winner takes it all, alright.
But does the loser
ever stand small?

Doesn't the loser even stand tall?
Likes of you decide, likes of me, abide. Is it? Is it?
No matter what,
let me face my Waterloo all by myself
tonight.

Tonight, a vivid carpet of the red Gul-mohur
has taken over the earth.
I am feeling quixotic--
it's for my childhood love's memory
and it definitely is for 'us', isn't it?

I think of the days when my hair was longer
and reveries were briefer;
and I then love my 'today' as
today it's the other way round.
Still, some pictures just get stuck
in the perpetual past
like those pluperfect lovers,
satiated with reminiscences and mothballs.
Like denoting an action
finalized prior to some remote past
of time oblique or time quantified.
Like an unsettled ornament confabbing with the ghost
of twilight.

Not bad if we can dust them from time to time
and then put them posterior
on our combined-concentration-mantlepiece, right?
We discover at times how we have taken over
what actually has fabled 'us'
and the here-and-now-you-and-me
to the utmost.

The Unending Road

We have come a long way love, a long way!
But the road to your heart is unending.
Well, I know, I can only strive to stride forth.

Imagine if there's a doppelganger for me to you!
Don't bury me, you know I am a seed.
From root to fruit, I will regrow, like eternal youth.

The seed brings out, indeed it recreates my creed--
the spirit of living-dying-dialectic. Playing with
stance and comment, my living voice is beneath.

And yes, how to misread a poem is not an easy binary to
considerately reading a poem. It is neither a negotiable
alternative
to confounding a poem to an uncluttered sheath.

I learnt early, if we want to feel tall,
we have to bow down. I am convinced that this poem
is a poem is a poem for you, though it can be a way to my breath.

Something is missing from all my glamorous glitzy
photographs—*myself*. Yet, this game of posturing to the world
I must maintain. The unending road to truth is rare and dearth.

The seed (that is me) knows if you are the soil, I would sow myself and grow.
Give me my share of love and shower on me.
I'll flower and sprout.
You may deliberate this as our unending truth.

This Monsoon

The symphony of shadows
in twilight's quiet arms,
where sun slips into dusk's gentle hands
the world breathes
and shadows play the chorus.
Colours soften, blend,
becoming shades of dreams.
The evening breeze whispers
its music through leaves
a melody for those who listen with their hearts.
The air, a canvas, brushed
with earth's snuffle, the scent of memory,
and each step on cool grass,
a whispered sonnet,
the heartthrob of the world.
Above, the moon, the silent poet,
unfurls silver verses, and stars flicker
distant candles stitching stories
in the fabric of the night.
The sky is historical, a 'period'.
Dreams pirouette
beneath this ancient, endless light.
In night's secret corners,
branches murmur to shadows.
The ecosphere is a book
each creature a storyteller

spinning tales in the language
of rustling leaves, dripping raindrops.

The night calls, drawing us inward,
where the commonplace turns
unusual, remarkable,
and time lets go, drifting
with the rhythm of stars.
In this sanctuary, souls have
calm camaraderie this monsoon,
heartbeats align with a cosmic pulse
a sacred communion of dreamers
held in night's quiet language
unstated by those who recognize silence.

Time is All We Have

My father believed, in the quiet tick of every passing second,
an opportunity unfolds, though it's often not reckoned.
Time, a river, time, a prospect, perpetual in its flow
carries our moments, both high and low.
The relic of time, his vintage wrist watch, a canvas anew
Tinted and ticked till his last breath, vibrant and true.
But one day the sun set, as certain as it did rise,
marking the end of life's quotidian camouflages.

He said, "Time is all we have"; it's the healer of lesions unseen,
it makes or mars, it softens the edges of what has been.
Yet, it whispers a truth we must heed,
because moments once lost become the moments in need.
In the heartbeats of life, both fast and slow
he repeated time's gentle reminder –it's precious, you know!
Cherish the present, for future is unsure,
and past is just a knowledge schema, a reminiscence pure.

In happiness and love, in sorrow and strife
time is the quantity unquantifiable of the physical life.
Time is the ability to be treasured, not squandered away
for each transitory microscopic moment is the signal of our stay.
Embrace the prized life that you have, count your blessings
bask in the cascade of time, revel in its showers.
Time is the thread that weaves us together,
an embroidery sheltered by providence forever.

Time was All He Had

Time was all he had, he knew, a truth so clear
an endless thread of worth, unremittingly near.
It inquests through his wristwatch, the relic of grandeur
a quiet, nostalgic witness to his life, pious and pure.
In morning's light and evening's shade,
time marched with him, though its paths had to fade.
It's in his reminiscence and in the tears
a constant companion through the years.

Values and morals gifted, a precious gem
in the summit of life, my father, a diadem.
He occupied his days astutely, never let them just pass
each choice he made, was certainly a looking glass.
Social commitment he had in every breath,
my illustrious father, who says that death is the only truth?
The world eulogizes him as time's eternal paragon
my rich pedigree, my timeless and eternal motivation.

Now time is watching me and my crusade
like a fleeting shadow, yet so profound.
I have to be his scrupulous, pedestrian daughter
for time was all he had and all I have, nothing less nothing more.
An endless sea, a door ajar, time the sovereign
is inviting me to live, love, to cherish infinitesimal.
I will hold it close, this vestige, this beacon, this gift divine,
in commemoration of my great father let it shine.

Time, the Relic

Time, the archive, settles like dust in the
immobile room of the past;
shadowed relics speak from silence
held to the earth yet reaching backward
drawn to stories waiting in obscurities.

A tarnished watch, banished hands
gestures lost in the hollow tick
each second a footprint
each hour a half-worn path to the past.
A locker lies closed
like a closed eye or a faded sun
inside it, pressed flowers
and soft faces locked in an embrace,
they linger there
bound in gold and quiet.

The pages of old letters turn
as if sighing words lifting from faded ink
brittle remnants of hands and voices
fingers tracing
the ink of ancient feeling.
A scarf rests, holding the shape of a presence
wrapped in scents of long-lost days
soft as the breath

of forgotten afternoons
keeping warmth as a memory would.

Each artifact, a vein in the quiet earth,
fragments woven by hands long gone
each piece, a thread in the pulse of time,
held by love's endless grip.
They wait in silence, as relics
in starlight that leaks through the dusk
in the pale thread of dawn's return
in the murmurs of the still night air
a time I dare not release
neither do I grope.

Waiting, in Synaesthesia

The planet shrinks when we grow up,
I just realized that.

And, of late,
time has been eating me, assembling
an agreeable little dent.

The house of wisdom says,
love and the risk of humiliation
go hand in hand.
But then, to live life through love
is the only way to go through it.

The mortification I mean.
Yes, the world runs on the whims,
chagrin and the caprices
of those who make one wait.

Waiting, I become wallflowers.
I am Erysimum of synaesthesia.

And now the book of wisdom,
again, just yet!

Synaesthesia, the neural condition,
causes me a consolidation of the senses,

colours allied to letters and numbers,
aromas and tastes to melody
or touch or vision.
Ah, the deadly sunlight is braying like a donkey.
the misanthrope's voice is a foul smell
that fades in a flicker.
Immense as the night.

True that, this indulgence of grief and waiting,
it's big as affluence and comfort.
The homeward kite smears off the fragrance
of sunshine from its annexes of the night.
I become slowly and gradually
a shrinking planet in waiting,
and a think-tank of delight.

What My Mother doesn't Know

What she doesn't know are shifting sand dunes,
waves of me breaking softly on her shore
my secrets hidden in the drift of provisional shelters
drawn close then washed away forever.
She cannot see the ache of my silken chains
how I wear the past like a woven cloak,
its weight appears as light as feathers after rain
but seamed with echoes, words I never spoke.
I ballet around the tales she'll never hear
my footsteps soft as snow that leave no trace
each secret, a bloom that won't bizarrely appear
rooted deep in some quiet, secret place.
Still, her love's a map I carry adjacent to my heart
a compass stamped in grace and edged with anxiety.

Women's Agency

In the weave, where the needle threads the
women's agency and lights a radiant spark
with courage that bends but never breaks,
they shape their fate, every path they take.
Unchained from the old, worn debate,
they stride through the world, undeterred by weight.
Dreams unbound, ambitions alight,
in their choices, their voices ignite.
Through trials and triumphs, they rise, they grow,
strength like rivers, steady in flow.
Their agency shines, a light in the night,
guiding them forward, bold and bright.
With hands that mould destiny's clay,
they forge a world where they hold sway.
United, they stand, with purpose in hand,
a force that shapes and reclaims the land.
Celebrating this power, untamed and true,
the essence of women, in all they pursue.
In their agency, they carve out space,
with grace and fire, they embrace their place.
And if the pen serves no purpose or plan,
then they cast it aside, let action span.

Your Intimate Skies

Ageing like fine wine is perfectly fine love,
but not in a basement, untouched.
There was solitude in my freedom
but never loneliness till we met.
I was stumbling around without any roots
as my door was forever shut.
But purposely I left some crack in there
so that one day you could get in with life and light.
To reject something, first you have to accept.
I knew this through the perception of insight.

Love, when we are born as human beings
are we not born with a responsibility?
Love makes us taller than who we are
yet, change is the only constant.
Thus, measuring the immeasurable and the immense
I merged with you immensely with delight.
Between live and love, the only difference is 'I'--
that is my grand imagination like a tempest.
Transgress the boundary of time
because with love, comes designs like secular humanism,
freedom, transcendentalism and human-right.
Feminism is not anathema, neither humanism,
love makes all things ethically correct.

Yet, love is the most disabling thing ever
because you reveal too much of yourself
and that is so very telling, isn't it?
In love, you have to lie to yourself; well, with time
you become a master of this art.
When you fall in love, it starts like good versus bad.
But as you peel the onion, it can be so different.

Not knowing to breathe the air that you didn't exhale
now I am going to the volatile lovers' zone with a molten heart.
Creating our own ecosystem, our heirloom,
I am creating a kind of civilizational text.
Love can be the authority of a king
with the accountability of a toddler-
eventually, love becomes a habit.
The habit ends. You die.
Death like hallucinations of a reverie, inappropriate and inept.
It's the trance of some other life lived elsewhere,
an enigma, a puzzle, a riddle, perplexing like mist.
The question is—how long does a love have to last
for the world to accept it as a trustworthy love-love—
not as a wizard conundrum of whodunit?
How long do the skies remain intimate?

The Difficult Daughter

I am her 'difficult daughter.'
Braiding her thin her hair in the mornings
fingers weaving through soft strands of silver,
each one a witness to years of care
of battles brawled and burdens agreed,
actually agreed and disagreed.
Pressing pain oil into her tired skin and knees
kneading out the weight of her worries,
the ones she never cultured
her indomitable spirit to share.
I love her,
fiercely
quietly
as the earth loves the roots that anchor it.

Well, then I am the storm she hardly sought.
I unsettle her calm with debriefings
that bloom like wildflowers in prohibited soil.
'Why must a daughter's worth
be measured in obedience?'
'Why must freedom feel like insurgence?'
'Why do you have to introduce me
ever so proudly, *Ah...she is my son!!*'
She does cringe
at the sharp edges of my tongue,
at the mirror I hold up,

shimmering more than she's ready to yield.
Her world is one of clear lines, easy binaries—
daughters must be daughters must be daughters.
Like
black-and-white etched in shingle.
Backgrounds folded neatly into the fabric of her life,
she clings to them,
as if they are the truths that keep her innocuous,
as if stepping beyond them
might unravel her entirely.
And
I am the thread she cannot rheostat.
I pull, I tug
tearing at the seams of her safe bet
a difficult daughter with dreams galore
that don't fit into her mount.

Her feet falter,
mine are the arms that steady her.
Her nights grow long and hushed,
mine is the voice that fills the void.
I am her detractor
and her keeper.
I am the challenger
when she is the climber.
Her co-voyager
her tough daughter
her confidante and crusader.
She doesn't understand
why I won't settle to mediocrity
why I refuse to shrink into the mould that
she carved with love and expectation.
And I
ache for the walls she won't let herself disrupt.

In the quiet moments,
when the urgings fade
and the light falls soft on her face,
I see the woman beneath the mother,
the girl she once was,
carrying the weight of a world that told her
to stay insignificant.
And I wonder if, in my defiance,
I am also fighting for her with her
for the freedom she never claimed,
for the voice she buried beneath her quiet.
Perhaps being difficult
is my only way of loving her,
of giving her what she cannot fight fit.
I stay,
the storm and the balm,
the critic and the concierge.
A daughter who is difficult
because love
sometimes
 is a messy, unyielding entity.

Two Cities

Delhi rises with a burst of ambition,
a city of restive horizons and steel spines.
The streets hum with a pace that crushes pauses
where history stands shoulder to shoulder with skyscrapers,
their shadows casting glory of a walled city.
In its veins runs a thirst—
for sovereignty, for acknowledgment,
for being the epicentre of the power-narrative.
Accommodative to all, flexible and inclusive,
the city of mosques and minarets
the city of dreams and triumphs.

Kolkata breathes in unhurried rhythms of joy,
a city wrapped in the perfume of measured
deliberate afternoons
and rain-soaked pages.
Here, history lingers like an old friend,
whispering Rabindra Sangeet through shaded alleys
and haunting the corners of coffee-stained *adda*.
The pulse is softer, its urgency muted
as if time knows it must wait here unhurried.

Delhi wears its intellect on starched collars
debating policy in boardrooms
the edifice futures in foundations.
A city of opportunities

it gleams with craft and weight.
It imparts ambition to dream in technicolour
but never overlooks to add a docket.

Kolkata cradles its intellect in the dusty folds of libraries
under dim lamps that flicker with poetry and protest.
Philosophy spills onto crumbling pavements
mingling with the scent of frying fish and brinjal or
potatoes with poppyseeds
and the sound of tram bells on weary rails.
Here, intellect doesn't climb, it rather meanders
weaving stories from the past
and questioning the future
 without necessitating answers.

Delhi's social fabric shimmers with contradictions:
a glamorous sheen of galas and gatherings
and the quiet struggles of those who build it.
It speaks in a thousand tongues,
yet never forgets to listen.
Cultural identity is a mosaic,
fractured but striving for unity.
Kolkata's soul lies in its unassuming congregations
the hum of shared meals and crowded book fairs.
Its festivals light up hearts before they light the streets
a city assured by shared love and laughter
and the rhythm of a collective heartbeat.
The past is not a shadow here
it is a cohort.
Delhi is the grand ambition of a dreaming nation,
a mirror of its struggles,
with imperfections in its own right.
It demands one to rise or be swept aside,
its fire is an invitation, caution and a delight.

Kolkata is the quiet rebellion of contemplation,
the lull of a lullaby that refuses to fade.
It doesn't mandate, it invites
to sit, to think,
to be content.
Two cities, two spirits, the door
left ajar in Delhi, to love and live,
opens in Kolkata, eclectic an alluring.
Two cities, one edgy, one weighty.
And somewhere in their alterations
they become two faces of my longing and belonging
to matter
to endure
to be conjured.

A Country Called Love

> *I took a sip and saw the vast ocean*
> *Wave upon wave caressed my soul.*
> *- Rumi*

Through deserts vast and cold
where twilight stretched its hands
 across the dust. Silence bore
the weight of broken dreams.

Through years of longing, shadows called
my name. Every road unravelled into mist
like a promise lost
in the breath of time.
The ocean held its secrets
in its depths, its waves reciting
echoes of the past. Distant hills stood
watching with knowing eyes.
Still I walked,
through valleys draped in night
where weary winds had whispered
tales of loss, and hope lay buried
deep beneath the pebbles.

A distant voice, a song upon the breeze
coming closer with each heart beat
an obvious presence like

the dawn's first golden spill,
a touch, a caress, a language
only the souls can state.

No border holds us captive
in agony. No map can mark
the way where we stand.

I have arrived, my wandering is done
in a country called love.

A country where I can trust people again--
that they won't disappear on me.
A country where there can be someone
to call my 'home'.
To be my future, past and present.
Someone who knows and loves
all the broken pieces in my heart.

A country where he is my prayer, he, the blessing.
He is the boon, he, benediction.
A country called love
from inception to prognosis.
From beginning to end.
A purposeful life
the door that was left open in the past
opened in the city of joy
in the country called 'love'.

Petrichor

Other than the petrichor springing
from the swiftly drying grass,
there is not a trace of evidence
that it had rained at all
nightlong.
Like iron that feasts on its crimson demise,
a silent assassin has happened in sombre skies.
Like rust destroying itself
on its own
time has been self-destructive.

Life, a candle that mourns its own flame,
dims in the dance of a self-created shame.
Save for the whispers the earth exhaled,
as dying grass in fragrance wailed,
no silver trail, no mirrored ground
to prove the storm had wept unbound.
Like a blade that drinks its own decay,
the crimson kiss of corrosion whispers its ruin,
so does life, a serpent devouring its tail,
unravels in the quiet art
of its own undoing.
And yes, the
petrichor redolent, that is the essence,
that is the lingering thing.

Letter to My Unborn Daughter

Tiny limbs smeared with my fresh enflamed blood
oozing out of the womb, gushing in fact.
I knew. I had lost you. Then and there. Shattered.
The sadomasochist burped, then casually farted, and snored

in a short while, when the maid rushed us to
the local hospital. I heard what you never uttered.
Ahh heal 'us', protect 'us', you and me, me and you,
Mom and her little girlie, wish to take the world in their stride.

Today, a letter to you, my unborn daughter, after
long two decades of quiet travail
telling our tales to your younger brother,
with a bleeding heart, I smile with exuding tears.

Smile to see my dream daughter alive in
her brother little; so full of love and compassion, so much a
feminist-humanist male, so strong to hold Mom's head high,
so much you, so as I would have you.

Ah! There was such rage over a female foetus
growing up to be a girl of power and conviction, like Mom dear.
Or like the Pancha Mahakanyas. And the marital rapes, the threats
to snatch you any given day, if I dissent; and then the termination.

If at all there is a next birth for you, my little fairy,
come back, come back to my womb, life minus you is so dreary.
You need not play the games that the heart must play.
Pledged before birth, you are not to be the woman of clay.

Like Ahilya, never fall prey to Indra's trickery; and if ever you do,
do it by your choice then, not anyone else's, neither
Goutama's nor Indra's.
Your penance need not be broken by Lord Rama, the one who
judged his wife; you need not regain your human form

by brushing his feet. Remain that dry stream, that stone,
till you find a way to my womb again, in another life, another Yug;
you need not be condoned of your guilt, you never were 'guilty'.
Let Indra be cursed, castrated, exposed by a thousand vulvae
that eventually turned into a thousand eyes. Or like
Draupadi, take your
birth from a fire-sacrifice,
be an incarnation of the fierce goddess Kali
or the goddess of wealth, Lakshmi;
but never be the sacrificial goat
to accept five husbands just because someone else deliberated.

If any Yudhishtir drops you at the Himalayas because you
loved Arjun more, look in his eyes and declare, loud and clear--
it's your right to live, love and pray. While never deriding
the Duryodhan and Karn of your destiny, live laudable my dear.

Nor Kunti be your role model; but if ever you propitiate the sage
Durvasa, who grants you a mantra to summon
a god and have a child by him, then take his charge.
Don't you recklessly test the boons life grants you by haze

nor invite the Sun-god, Surya, give birth to Karn, and abandon.
An unborn child is better than the one dejected, forlorn.
Or if ever you are Tara, the apsara, the celestial nymph,
who rises from the churning of the milky ocean

be the Tara, Sugriva's queen and chief diplomat,
the politically correct one, the woman in control of herself
and folks around. In the folk Ramayanas,
Tara casts a curse on Rama by the supremacy of her chastity,

while in some versions, Rama enlightens Tara. Be her, the absolute.
Or be Mandodari, the beautiful, pious, and righteous.
Ravana's dutiful wife who couldn't be his guiding force,
Bibhishana's compliant wife, the indomitable grace.

Be you, the elemental, candid, real woman who is my ideal.
Don't ever let another female foetus be the victim of
sadomasochism, unlike your fragile, fledgling Mom.
Be all that she could never be, be her role model.

I send you my prayers, the prayer before birth.
Moon, rain, oceans, and the blue firmament,
shining stars and a sun aglow are all that I have--
you must call them your own, my unborn daughter.

Forgive me my love, for you died with all the petals
falling from my autumny breast, the breast that you never suckled;
you rain on my being and burn my heart, but calm my soul
like simmering snow slowly concealed yet revealed.

You will stay indomitable, taking new lives every single day
in Mom's prayers, poetry, social responsibilities, ecofeminism,
messages, voices, layers of thoughts and action. My girl,
I am what I decided to be after losing you, that's the euphemism.

I am not just a woman since that fateful night, but entire
womankind. Now I am a woman of full circle,
within me there is the
power to create, nurture and transform.
I rediscover pieces of myself
through your unborn narrative,
in the resonance of my quirky confluence.

The *Akshyayapatra* in Jagannath Puri

In a kitchen where the flames ignite,
a symphony of manna-like taste takes flight.
The pots and pans of the Supakar, the chef's delight
create a world of pure epicurean gourmet.

With earthen pots donned and wooden ladles in hand
a culinary dance of the temple-chef
like the Chaiti-Ghoda, intrepid and grand.
Ingredients blend, a nicely-choreographed band
creating dishes from a far-off indigenous land.

From ecofriendly spices and turmeric
that stimulate the dormant senses
to herbs that lend their fragrant tenses
here cooking is a gift, like Draupadi's, like Sita's,
without pretences
a journey through life's varied lenses.

A surge of love, a smidgin of conservation of the Mahaprasad
in every meal, a story of food and livestock to share.
From earthen hearths to the puja mandap
a journey rare, never-ending food's alchemy, beyond compare.

Sautéing, simmering and boiling green, organic food
with techniques old and techniques newfangled.
In every recipe, a folktale to tell, an archive, a lost-world to view
a voyage of flavours, consecration, like a dream come true.

The enchant that Mahaprasada brings
in every nook and cranny
the love among the devotees beyond margins
a canvas of a borderless society, a masterpiece uncanny
in a kitchen where traditions, cultures melt, thrive and pulse.

Where ancient wisdoms, Indian knowledge systems
stir in every dish
indigenous gifts of the old-world, the textile of intertextual dreams
from North to South, from East to Western shores
Zara Shabara's tribe and their culinary treasures.

Here, secret recipes are passed down, oral voices speak
beneath the moon of the Puri sea-beach, in the gentle light
and dark.
The aroma of cedar and sage in planks and earthen pots so right
a salmon coral story in cedar wraps does proliferate.

A taste of history, Shabara tribes' journey to Puri badadanda,
Odia Monarch Indradyumna and tribal king Vishvavasu —
their legend.
The mythopoetic and the mythopoeia of the creation of
the Jagannath temple, the story of the cosmological time's sand.

Lord Jagannath, the Lord of the Universe, His pitch-black skin
His half-formed limbs, His solidarity with the 'Black' and the
differently-abled;
the morphological features and countenance of an unfinished,
premature, aboriginal, 'savage', exotic look of the three deities.

Three siblings' kitchen garden that Goddess Laxmi embellishes,
brinjal, beans, radish unite companions in the soil. Spirits entwine
in harmony, they cultivate hope, their colours optimistic.
Food is the theme, food-culture is the symbol of the land,
of life's musical design.

Food is the sacred art in Lord Jagannath's Rasoi-Ghara,
here ethos and faith work as the fuel, ancestral secrets whispered.
Inherited moods guide the cook's deft hand
in ghee, zero-oil, steamed-vegetables,
honey and beans, histories unfold.

From ancient rituals, tastes nostalgic, poignant.
A journey back through time, to that sacred home of the Lord.
From Pacific Ocean and islands to the desert's heat,
aboriginal recipes, a tradition to complete,
in every bite, there's antiquity.

No one goes famished, starving from Jagannath Puri.
Here, food is the language that transcends all borders.
A taste of Odia ethos, food is the world of divine orders.
In every bite, a feeling hoards memories,
emotions and life's rewards.

Prof. Nandini Sahu, Vice Chancellor, Hindi University, West Bengal, the Amazon Bestselling Author, is a major voice in contemporary Indian English literature. She has accomplished her doctorate in English literature under the guidance of Late Prof. Niranjan Mohanty, Prof. of English, Visva Bharati, Santiniketan. She has been widely published in India, U.S.A, U.K., Africa, Italy, Australia and Pakistan. Apart from numerous other literary awards, she is a triple gold medalist in English literature; she has received the Gold Medal from the hon'ble Vice-President of India for her contributions to English Studies in India in the year 2019. She is the recipient of the prestigious Michael Madhusudan Academy Award-2024,Lifetime Achievement Award (SAFE)-2024 and Tagore Samman-2025(Mukradhara). She is the author and editor of twenty-three books, *The Other Voice, Recollection as Redemption, The Post-Modernist Delegation to English Language Teaching, The Post Colonial Space: Writing the Self and the Nation, Silver Poems on My Lips, Folklore and the Alternative Modernities* (Vol.I), *Folklore and the Alternative Modernities* (Vol. II), *Sukamaa and Other Poems, Suvarnarekha, Sita(A Poem)(2014), Dynamics of Children's Literature, Zero Point, Selected Poems of Nandini Sahu(Winter-2020), Selected Poems of Nandini Sahu(Spring-2021), Re-reading Jayanta Mahapatra, A Song,Half & Half , Shedding the Metaphors, Collected Poems of Nandini Sahu, Collected Poems of Niranjan Mohanty, Hindu Studies: Foundations and Frameworks , Sita(A Long Narrative Poem)(2025)* and *Medusa*(A Collection of Poems). She is the Former Director, School of Foreign Languages, Professor of English at Indira Gandhi National Open University [IGNOU], New Delhi, India, is currently the Vice Chancellor, Hindi University, West Bengal,. Her areas of research interest cover Indian Literature, New Literatures, Indigenous Knowledge Systems, Hindu Studies, American Literature, Folk Literature, Children's Literature and Critical Theory. She is the Chief Editor/Founder Editor of *Interdisciplinary Journal of Literature and Language* (IJLL), a bi-annual peer-reviewed journal in English. Professor Sahu has designed multiple academic programmes on Folklore and Culture Studies, American Literature, Postcolonial Literatures, British Poetry, Children's Literature and Indian Philosophical Thoughts for IGNOU and many other universities.

www.kavinandini.blogspot.in
www.nandinisahu.in
https://drnandinisahusita.blogspot.com/
www.professornandinisahusita.blogspot.com
Addresses:
Prof Nandini Sahu
Vice Chancellor, Hindi University, West Bengal
nandinisahu.vchindiuniversity@gmail.com
&
Prof.Nandini Sahu
Professor of English
Former Director, School of Foreign Languages,IGNOU
New Delhi-110068, India.
E-mail: kavinandini@gmail.com
nandinisahu@ignou.ac.in
Mobile: 09811991539

Black Eagle Books

www.blackeaglebooks.org
info@blackeaglebooks.org

Black Eagle Books, an independent publisher, was founded as a nonprofit organization in April, 2019. It is our mission to connect and engage the Indian diaspora and the world at large with the best of works of world literature published on a collaborative platform, with special emphasis on foregrounding Contemporary Classics and New Writing.

www.ingramcontent.com/pod-product-compliance
Lightning Source LLC
Chambersburg PA
CBHW060616080526
44585CB00013B/847